PLATFORM PAPERS

QUARTERLY ESSAYS ON THE PERFORMING ARTS

No. 22
October 2009

CURRENCY HOUSE

PLATFORM PAPERS
Quarterly essays from Currency House Inc.
Editor: Dr John Golder, j.golder@unsw.edu.au

Currency House Inc. is a non-profit association and resource centre advocating the role of the performing arts in public life by research, debate and publication.

Postal address: PO Box 2270, Strawberry Hills, NSW 2012, Australia

Email: info@currencyhouse.org.au   Tel: (02) 9319 4953
Website: www.currencyhouse.org.au   Fax: (02) 9319 3649

Editorial Board: Katharine Brisbane AM, Dr John Golder, John McCallum, Martin Portus, Greig Tillotson

ISBN 978-0-9805632-4-5
ISSN 1449-583X
Typeset in 10.5 Arrus BT
Printed by Hyde Park Press, Richmond, SA

This edition of Platform Papers is supported by the Keir Foundation, the Greatorex Foundation, Neil Armfield, David Marr, Joanna Murray-Smith and other individual donors and advisers. To them and to all our supporters Currency House extends sincere gratitude.

Contents

AVAILABILITY *Platform Papers*, quarterly essays on the performing arts, is published every January, April, July and October and is available through bookshops or by subscription. For order form, see page 72.

LETTERS Currency House invites readers to submit letters of 400–1,000 words in response to the essays. Letters should be emailed to the Editor at info@currencyhouse.org.au or posted to Currency House at PO Box 2270, Strawberry Hills, NSW 2012, Australia. To be considered for the next issue, the letters must be received by 14 November 2009.

CURRENCY HOUSE For membership details, see our website at: www.currencyhouse.org.au

Copyright, Collaboration and the Future of Dramatic Authorship

BRENT SALTER

The author

Brent Salter is Visiting Research Fellow in the Law School of Macquarie University, having graduated there in 2006 with First Class Honours and the University Medal. He has published extensively in Australia and internationally on the intersection between the law and the arts, and at present holds an appointment as Legal Research Officer to the High Court of Australia in Canberra, 2010–11. On completion he will commence doctoral studies in the United States on a comparative history of theatrical authorship and the law in several countries, from both an interdisciplinary and a doctrinal perspective. The copyright issues discussed in this essay are central to his ongoing research.

Acknowledgements

I should like to thank the following theatre practitioners for their passionate and candid involvement in this research. Each of them was generous both with their time and in allowing their comments to be published here. All the quotations that are otherwise unacknowledged in the text, therefore, are from the interviews I conducted with David Berthold, Rob Brookman, Brendan Cowell, Gale Edwards, John Frost, Rachel Healy, Nick Marchand, Tommy Murphy, Gino Principe, Alana Valentine, Ben Winspear, Tom Wright—and with one playwright who prefers to remain anonymous. A special, indirect thank-you to Edward Albee, who devoted a lunch break to discussing the issues raised here.

This research has evolved over three stages—don't all the best stories turn on the number three?—and each has benefited from the generous support of friends and colleagues. I wish to thank Dr Katherine Biber and Dr Nicole Graham for their guidance during the early stages of the project. Professor Kathy Bowrey provided insightful commentary, as it began to grow. It was she who opened my mind to the limitless places to which my research might lead me in the future. Katherine, Nicole and Kathy, in terms of professional generosity and collegiality you set the kind of high benchmark to which all young academics should aspire.

In the final stages of this Platform Paper, I am grateful to Dr Mark Williams, a specialist in arts law and intellectual copyright, who kindly read a draft and made some valuable suggestions. Finally, I would like to extend my warmest gratitude to Dr John Golder for editing the work. It has been a rare and incredibly rewarding experience to work with such an engaged and committed editor. Courage, mon brave John!

Although this essay owes much to all those mentioned above, and others too numerous to mention, the responsibility for any glaring errors that may remain is solely mine.

Introduction

I n a heated exchange with director Danny Mann
at the 1992 Inge Festival in Kansas, playwright
Edward Albee succinctly articulated what he saw
as the relationship between the playwright and his
director:

> ALBEE: Theatre is not merely the furnishing of
> pleasure or fun. It's engagement of thought, of
> self, of mind.
>
> MANN: But it has to have emotion. The play *has*
> to have emotion. And the director has to add it,
> handle it; he has to help actors to deliver emotion.
> The director determines and defines what emotions
> should be included in the play. When you direct,
> you want the audience's participation—which has
> to do with emotion, not just with cerebration, not
> just thought or idea!
>
> ALBEE: [*strenuously objecting*] A first-rate play's text
> has *not* just cerebral ideas; it has *all* the emotions
> right there! In a great play, the playwright does
> *not* need the director's 'help'. The good director
> translates what is already there in the play; he does
> not have to *create* it in a first-rate play. It's in the
> subtext.[1]

Having waged numerous battles over the previous four
decades in order to assert his authorial rights over his

plays—including several attempts to close productions of the Pulitzer Prize-winning *Who's Afraid of Virginia Woolf* [2]—Albee sees the playwright as the authorial source, and therefore the original rights holder, commanding ultimate authority over it. For him there is a clear distinction between the 'creative act' and the 'interpretative act'. In his view, directors, designers, actors etc. do not create: it is their job to interpret what the writer has created. Without his original work, they would have no function at all. If anything, Albee's position appears to have hardened with age: earlier this year he said that his advice to the playwright, new or established, working in the American theatre was to tell every other theatre worker, 'Go fuck yourself!' [3]

Legally in the United States—and in most respects this is mirrored in Australia—a copyright framework has been constructed which gives Albee every right to assert his authority over his original dramatic work. In Australia, copyright protects authors of works, including dramatic works, by virtue of Part 3 of the Australian *Copyright Act 1968* (Cth). [4] The copyright owner and the original author are not necessarily the same person, but it is usually the case that the writer is the first owner of the copyright. [5] For all that, in the more than 500 pages that constitute the *Copyright Act*, the word 'playwright', the actual author of a dramatic work, is never once to be found. Nevertheless, the *Copyright Act* and the courts have constructed a framework whereby dramatic-work authorship is defined by a fundamental requirement that ideas be expressed in material form. Put another way, rewards go to those individuals whose work consists in producing tangible material—what will be referred to in this essay as 'fixed' and 'static' material—as opposed to artists who operate in a 'fluid' and ephemeral way. It is a legal framework that has been used to minimise the number of original-authorial contributions.[6]

They might not rate a mention in the *Act*, but unlike directors and other 'non-writer collaborators' in text-based theatre,[7] playwrights do record the results of their creative output in material form. Consequently, in most cases they are considered the original authors and enjoy the benefits the *Act* provides, benefits that include the right to exploit the work[8] and concomitant ownership rights.[9] By contrast, collaborators such as directors, who make a significant artistic contribution to the realisation of the original work, do not enjoy the same financial benefits. Directors and actors are paid a wage or else a negotiated fee. The playwright, on the other hand, receives no such fee or wage, only his royalty cheque, which is a percentage of the box-office receipts his work has attracted.

Tensions between writer and non-writer collaborators are not new, though they have been in the news in recent times. Over the last two decades a number of disputes have played out in the press and the courts, commanding the attention of journalists and legal scholars in both Australia[10] and America;[11] and their prevailing line of argument challenges Albee's hard distinction between the playwright as creator and the non-writer collaborator as interpreter. In light of a number of public disputes between non-writer collaborators and canonical playwrights, or the estates of canonical playwrights, more and more commentators have argued that the current framework is problematic and/or there is a need for greater recognition in copyright law of the contributions made by non-writer theatre collaborators.[12] Industry-based contracting practices that acknowledge the work of non-writer contributors are seen as the first step towards the legal recognition of a collaborative theatrical right to dramatic authorship.

This essay steps away from the doctrinal debate over the construction of original dramatic authorship, in order to consider ethnographically, at an initial level of inquiry, the operation of the current copyright framework. Apart from exploring the impact of copyright law on theatre practitioners, the essay pays attention to the economic issue of *ongoing* rewards: are those who continue to bring the play to the stage after the initial production adequately rewarded under the current arrangements? Examining some of the complexities surrounding the operation of ongoing rewards is a useful way in which to better understand the actual economic and creative control a playwright has over their work in practice.

What follows needs to be read with certain conditions in mind. Space restrictions preclude me from examining the issue of moral rights in the depth it demands. Both before and after the enactment of moral rights legislation in 2000, moral rights issues have indirectly emerged in Australian disputes, and been widely reported in the press, but settled before formal litigation. In particular, the issue of the 'integrity' of an original work would have been relevant to the dispute over both the 1996 Sydney Theatre Company production of David Williamson's *Heretic*, and Company B Belvoir's 2003 production of Samuel

Beckett's *Waiting for Godot*;[13] of which more later. It should also be noted that this essay constitutes a first step towards a much larger, international examination of copyright and the playwright, to be undertaken as a doctoral dissertation over the next few years. Sample sizes, therefore, are small and distinctions drawn, between, say, profit and non-profit organisations, are tentative. Furthermore, some of the interviews with theatre practitioners were conducted three years ago, when I first began to take an interest in these issues. Nonetheless, the essay offers an insight into some of the complexities surrounding the operations of dramatic authorship and suggests that there is good reason to re-examine the rationale behind any amendment of the current copyright framework and its present protection of the writer.

1

The writer and the 'creative act'

When the American playwright Craig Lucas agreed to his *Prayer for My Enemy* being premiered Off-Broadway by the non-profit Roundabout Theatre Company as part of their 2008-2009 season, he had no idea he was walking into a legal minefield.[14] The standard originating-producer agreement, he quickly discovered, required him to sign over to Roundabout no less than 40 per cent of author royalties from productions of his play—for the next ten years.

Lucas knew that all non-profit theatres required a percentage of a playwright's future earnings. Indeed, industry-based 'subsidiary right' agreements between originating producers and playwrights have a long tradition in the non-profit theatre, both overseas and in Australia. Rob Brookman, general manager of Sydney Theatre Company (STC), explains the rationale behind the agreements which, in Australia, usually entitle originating producers to one or two per cent of future playwright royalties:

> Some playwrights are highly collaborative and find it quite difficult to write in a vacuum. Others are much more inclined to deliver a script that is to all intents and purposes finished—and then we just polish it. Others will deliver something that is really like the carcass of the script, then filled in through the workshopping process. So there are very different work processes. But whichever way you [go], there can be a significant investment of time, place, money, people, resources that are both tangible and intangible. And then there is [the question of] the courage that any producer has to have to take the risk on a brand new piece. So the [requirement that] there be some potential return to the producer is a just one.

Agreements for an originating-producer royalty rely on a significant level of trust between the playwright, the originating producer and subsequent producer. Under the Australian Writer's Guild general agreement, upon which many production companies model their own agreements, playwrights place themselves under an 'ethical' obligation to make 'reasonable efforts' to ensure that the originating producer agreement is honoured. This can sometimes be difficult to enforce, as director David Berthold has pointed out:

> Often the playwright has made reasonable efforts and will be able to get the extra percentage from the subsequent production of the play. And when they couldn't do that, often they take it out of their own royalty. [...] It does depend on a level of trust on the part of the writer's agent to actually make that effort and the writer's agent has to push the subsequent producer to honour that part, so of course that doesn't always happen. It's still a flawed mechanism and [...] can only work if everyone agrees to it and actually sees it as a fundamental part of how we make productions, and then how [playwrights] are given second and third rights. But that agreement is not there at the moment.

As Berthold says, subsequent producers may need to be 'pushed' to honour the agreement. Any subsequent producer will not have been a party to the original agreement, so 'the originating-producer royalty does depend ultimately on the goodwill of the second and third and fourth producer'.

What startled Craig Lucas was the figure of 40 per cent, which, however standard it was for commercial productions in the United States, he regarded as far too high for a non-profit production. So he took the extraordinary step of moving his play from Roundabout to Playwright Horizons, who were willing to produce it at only ten per cent of future earnings. By doing so, Lucas rekindled a long-simmering larger debate regarding the level of control a playwright should have over their original work in an art form that is inherently collaborative: control over the percentage of original royalties, and creative control of the original work that is produced and control over other's freedom to exploit the work in future productions. 'The profession of playwright in today's American theatre', says award-winning playwright Richard Nelson, 'is under serious attack [...] from those who want "to help".' He believes that a culture has developed whereby the playwright has become, increasingly and involuntarily, dependent on the contribution of non-writer collaborators in order to realise the play. No matter what a playwright writes, or rewrites, the task of finally bringing the play to the stage is too big, too complex, too demanding of talents and skills, for him to achieve on his own. Writers have no alternative but to accept that, 'if they wish to participate in a process that perhaps will lead to the production of their work, then this will require rewriting and revision guided and cajoled by others', and therefore that 'the onus for change is not on the playwright but on others'.[15]

The Craig Lucas case is a good example of an issue that is often overlooked by legal commentators consumed by critiquing the technical limitations of a copyright system that is defined in fixed and individual terms. Copyright is as much about a power relationship between collaborators as it is about creative contribution. This essay will illustrate that for every Craig Lucas or Edward Albee who may have the authority to assert their legal rights, there are countless other playwrights who do not enjoy this luxury. However, it will also be argued that, while serious conflict between collaborators is an infrequent occurrence in the Australian theatre community, we must look beyond the isolated and very public instances of such conflict and consider the impact that any compromise of playwrights' intellectual property rights will have on the vast majority of writers—writers whose names are not Albee, or Beckett, or Williamson. It therefore presents a counterpoint to the dominant position held in academic commentary, and challenges the ability of the current copyright framework to adequately recognise the collaborative nature of theatrical authorship.

The enduring individual-author narrative

Most of the literature on playwrights' interaction with copyright law is confined to the experiences of established playwrights, who have more opportunities than emerging playwrights to see their work professionally produced.[16] So it is to the emerging playwright that I want first to turn, in order to document her experiences. The theatrical disputes that are reported in the public papers tend to involve writers who have lucrative careers, who have earned substantial royalties from multiple productions of their plays over time. The success of the small number of established Australian playwrights—let us not pretend that there are more than a handful who are able to sustain a living exclusively on the income from royalty cheques—tends to overshadow the struggles of lesser-known figures.

Let me start by looking at the enduring legacy of the current legal framework that prioritises individual theatre creators who reduce their work to expressed ideas in a material form. There are, I believe, three compelling reasons to preserve the current individual authorship model. First, the individual model continues to have a strong influence on many theatre practitioners, including non-writer collaborators. Secondly, playwrights are a particularly vulnerable group who deserve protection. And thirdly, under the current copyright model, the vast majority of productions appear to function harmoniously. In other words, why change a winning formula?

Cambridge law professor Lionel Bently provides a pragmatic, and widely acknowledged, justification for why the individual-based copyright model has endured. If copyright law has evolved around the individual, it is because commercially it has always been easier to simplify the framework with regard to individuals who produce their works in material form:

> In cases of collaborative works, [copyright law] frequently refuses to recognise contributors as authors in an attempt to simplify ownership. Because a single property owner means that assignments and licenses of copyright are easier and cheaper to effect, copyright law prefers to minimise the number of authorial contributions it is prepared to acknowledge rather than reflect the realities of collaborative authorship.[17]

Aside from these pragmatic reasons, it is also important to acknowledge the continuing hold that the individual-author narrative has on modern-day playwrights. The concerns raised by Richard Nelson with regard to the possible impact on the ways in which a writer might go about writing, or ways in which a work gets written, are shared by many writers. They were raised in 1997 during the United States case of *Thomson v Larson*, in which the free-lance dramaturg Lynn M. Thomson, who teaches at New York University, made a claim of statutory authorship of Jonathan Larson's hit Broadway musical *Rent*. Hired to assist Larson on the New York Theatre Workshop production, she claimed authorship of almost 50 per cent of the musical's book and nine per cent of the lyrics. While several legal scholars sided with Thomson, members of New York City's New Dramatists, a non-profit centre for the promotion of talented new writers, vigorously defended Larson's right to be regarded as the sole author. As Devorah Katz explained in a recent paper, even though Thomson was found by the court to have 'contributed significant copyrightable portion to the end result', *Rent* 'had not been a joint work'.[18] Meanwhile the position of the New York City's New Dramatists was eloquently articulated thus:

> True authorship is intensely idiosyncratic and personal. It lies in the act of transforming the raw material of one's own experience into art. A play like *Long Day's Journey into Night* might be admirable for its Aristotelian unities, and the clarity of each character arc. But what makes it inevitably, inextricably Eugene O'Neill's play is something far more

primary: its author grew up battling consumption, an alcoholic father and a morphine addicted mother and he recapitulated that experience in the form of a play. [...] To suggest that the editorial contributions of its director, dramaturg or cast are tantamount to O'Neill's own achievement is to diminish the very nature of his art. [...]

The most ephemeral but distinctive tool a writer possesses is an authorial voice. A writer's voice is as individual and marked as a thumbprint, and is a playwright's truest imprimatur. It is as innate as breathing, and can be as unique as any genetic code. By its very singular nature, it is seldom born in the act of collaboration. True authorial voice always pre-dates the first rehearsal of a text. And it is—and will always be—an author's most distinguishing and valuable feature. Therein lies the true nature of authorship, and no other party can lay claim to it.[19]

Sydney playwright Alana Valentine agrees: by virtue of being the one who first embarks on the creative and risky process, and who sets her own name upon the ultimate product, the playwright is the only collaborator who deserves the reward of ownership:

It all goes back to that staring at a blank page that so many people in the other collaborative places don't ever have to do, and that's why authors get so thingy [about ownership]. If you go home and type up the scene at the end of the day, then, yeah, we can probably share copyright, but if you don't, then [that scene's] still just existing in the ether as a good idea. It's the writer who takes all the filaments and weaves them into something coherent.

In considering changes to ownership structures, commentators also tend to overlook the enduring influence of the individual-author narrative on many practitioners. Some believe that younger playwrights generally have a more collaborative understanding of their work. 'Younger writers have a different attitude towards text,' says actor / director Ben Winspear:

> I think [that] if you grow up with post-modernist and deconstructed approaches to text and can see ways to pull it apart, look through it, explode it, kind of cut and paste, it's like a younger appreciation of text is […] more varied and more open for interaction. I think a lot of the writers who were brought [up] in the days when companies were—and to a large degree they still are—in pursuit of the great Aussie classic, they are striving for this goal each time and often end up writing for reasons which are tied up with ego and career rather than theatrical possibility.

On the other hand, the experience of former general manager of Company B Belvoir, Rachel Healy, has been that younger playwrights were open to the collaborative processes involved in bringing their play to production, but others held firmly to their role as the authorial source of both the text and its meaning:

> Certainly, when some young playwrights work [with Company B], and in particular when they are working with Neil [Armfield], they don't defer to his experience and reputation. We've had lots of young playwrights […] who are very feisty, very clear about what they want to achieve and […] decisive about what they want their play to do.

Where those I interviewed did concur was in the case of text-based drama: the individual authorial voice had to be protected. Alana Valentine was strong in her defence of *Run Rabbit Run*, her 2004 verbatim play about the South Sydney football club:

> I just see [the way I create] as an incredibly skilled job and that's why it says 'by Alana Valentine'. It doesn't say 'by Alana Valentine and the South Sydney community', because it was […] my version of the story and that benefits both of us. If they don't like it, then it's Alana Valentine's take on it, not theirs. Also I think it [counteracts] that notion that I'm somehow representing a universal story that just exists out there and I just have to go and catch it. It's not true. I have to go and create it and I absolutely would defend the fact that, once I type up what they've said to me, that is my copyright. […] People tell stories until you can't listen, but I typed it up, so I think it's mine.

During the production of *Stolen*, Jane Harrison's first play, the playwright was acknowledged by her colleagues as a very collaborative writer: the stage-manager remembered that '[a]t the first reading, Jane said to the cast and director: "It's yours. It doesn't belong to me." [Despite the fact that she knew] we ha[d] recorded scenes and added and taken out a considerable amount.' Harrison explained that she had adopted a more collaborative approach because the work, about five Aboriginal people from the 'stolen generations', was a co-operative project. It had been commissioned in 1992 by the Ilbijerri Theatre Co-operative. However, despite having 'handed the play over' to her cast at the start of rehearsals, she now maintains that the director and dramaturg had not told her in advance just how substantial the changes to her original text might be. As a result, she insisted on her right to be regarded as its sole author:

> I thought [the play] would just be tweaked. [... However,] scenes were workshopped when I wasn't present, the dramaturg worked with the actors and I remember on about the third day her handing me some stuff that she'd written. I'm glad that at that stage I [...] had the courage to say: 'Hang on, why are *you* writing this?' She said: 'Well, that's what a dramaturg does.' And I said: 'No, I am the writer. Give me the ideas, but I will write them.' I'm glad I did that at that stage because I think it made it more clear-cut. Yes, they could improvise scenes or whatever she could feed in [the way of] ideas, [...] but then [they should] show them to me. The words on the page were mine. I'm aware of how collaborative it is and I'm aware that so many other people contributed along the way, but I feel the final choice of the words was my responsibility.

Playwright Tommy Murphy echoes these sentiments: 'Just [as] the lighting designer makes sure that the light looks wonderful, the stage manager makes sure that the light doesn't fall on someone's head, that's their responsibility. [...] My responsibility is to make sure that the words are good. I feel that I have ownership over that. Even if there might be a lot of other people's ideas, it's my responsibility to have the final say over them.'

Several of the producers interviewed also strongly identified with this individual-author narrative and were acutely aware of the challenges that playwrights faced. The stark contrast between originating-producer agreements in the United States and Australia illustrates this sensitivity. Standard Australian contractual practice suggests that the originating producer is unable to cut into the playwright's royalty—or receive a greater percentage of the gross box-office—until the play has earned for itself a further production or two, and the playwright has earned a certain amount of income through his royalty—a situation that is hardly likely to arise very often in the case of new Australian plays. As Rob Brookman says, 'In a way I wish that [these agreements] became problematic more often, because that would indicate that more productions were actually being picked up rapidly, in the wake of being first produced. The sorry truth is that the majority of new plays [...] get put on once and then don't see the light of day again.'

On the individual-author narrative Brookman has this to say:

> I believe in the playwright as the creative force and primary imagination that creates the work. The contribution of others along the way may or may not assist, as the playwright has the right to accept or reject the ideas. [Once accepted,] the ideas become the playwright's. If there is an agreement up front about investment that is made in the play, I have no argument about sharing royalties. [...T]hat's a straightforward commercial deal. What doesn't work for me is the idea that *post facto* people might lay claim to a proportion of the copyright! [...] Playwrights as a group must be amongst the worst-paid and worst-treated in the world.

2

'My right to write':
the vulnerable author

Commentary that charges ahead with a reform agenda often emphasises the limitations of the current framework, but fails to consider what that framework protects. Tommy Murphy, author of *Holding the Man*, believes that, since most original works are unlikely to be given more than one professional production, it is important to protect the playwright's financial interests. It is, after all, with the name of the playwright, and not that of any collaborator, that the play is likely to be associated in the public mind:

> Say I was upset with a professional production of my play and I felt I hadn't been consulted [about changes made by collaborators]. What I would be concerned about is the fact that in Australia that's likely to be the sole production of my play. In some ways the production [carries] more weight in Australia, because we don't reproduce our plays enough. [...T]hat one production [might be] the only life that play [has]. When the review's in the *Sydney Morning Herald*, it's me who's blamed when the work sucks, [...] so it seems that I should have the benefit of also owning that work.

Apart from issues relating to reputation and lack of financial reward, the act of writing itself can be a long and isolating experience that often entails years of research, workshopping and script development before something resembling a completed work begins to emerge. Nor does an extensive period of development guarantee a professional production. '[Y]ou ought to try taking the risk to be a full-time professional playwright', said Alana Valentine. 'That's a 20-year risk with your life. […] I mean, that's investing in yourself for 20 years on the basis that nothing might come of it.'

In light of such uncertainty, playwrights are bound to be anxious about a copyright system that extended original ownership rights to non-writer collaborators. The producers here also stated that it was rare for a playwright, even a well-established one, to be given an additional fee on top of their ten per cent royalty of box-office takings. Alana Valentine reflects Edward Albee's views and emphasises the point that what is really at issue is subsequent productions of a text:

> Copyright is about selling it on, isn't it? [… Y]ou want copyright so that you can sell it on to someone else. Well, why would the artistic director of a company who has a full-time job need to sell it on? Why do the actors who get work on subsequent shows that the writer is not involved in need copyright? It's a protection of the [playwright's] rights.

In addition, although most of the producers interviewed are supportive of playwrights, amongst some emerging playwrights there is a genuine concern that, if they did not have protection under copyright law, established collaborators could take both financial and artistic advantage. Some of the playwrights interviewed had experienced such challenging situations.

One such writer, who wished to remain anonymous, outlined some of the pressures involved in dealing with theatre companies:

> If it was a state theatre company, you [would be] well aware that was a really rare opportunity and it would be a really difficult situation [to decide whether to compromise your rights]. On the one hand you have the integrity of the work, and on the other hand you are having to work around a whole lot of other people's needs. [...I]t would be a very hard thing to resist. There has to be negotiation between both parties. I think that is really crucial. I would probably have to have that understanding from the beginning of the job.

The fear always exists that, if the playwright does not consent to changes, then the producer may choose d their work. In a circumstance of unequal bargaining power between an emerging playwright and a large professional theatre company, there is a risk that the playwright's legal rights could end up being negligible. And, further, if her play went into production and she felt that she was being asked to make changes under duress, the playwright might well feel compelled not to enforce their rights. After all, few new playwrights would have the funds to commence formal litigation and, if they did, they might fear future reprisals from the theatre community.

John Frost, managing director of the Gordon/Frost Organisation, one of the leading producers of live theatre in Australia, affirms the commercial realities. It is imperative, he says, for the producer to take a hands-on role:

> If I knew that I was going to have an author that
> was a pain [...]—I probably wouldn't have employed
> them anyway [if] I couldn't get my way in having
> my piece pushed across. [S]ay I did have an author
> that was a pain [...] I would have to confront that
> quite rigorously. I wouldn't just sit back and think
> 'OK, well, that's it, because that's what he's written.'
> I would definitely want an input.

Many playwrights, says Alana Valentine, would be
prepared to forego financial reward altogether to
have their play produced by a state theatre. After all,
such opportunities don't occur every day. Ultimately,
however, she believes any relationship based on a
significant power imbalance is unsustainable:

> [Young playwrights] would do it for nothing. [...]
> You can do that to young writers [...], but you'll
> turn around in ten years and it will be: 'Well, where
> are the writers?' Well, you know where they are,
> they are working for insurance companies because
> ... why wouldn't you? Excuse me, but what is the
> deal for staying in the industry and becoming really
> good at what you do and having a voice and not
> just telling stories, but reflecting the spirit, and the
> concerns of our times? Who pays you to be doing
> that all the time? Who pays you for your vision?
> What that is, is your copyright. I often feel quite
> angry that sometimes companies will advertise a
> competition [with an award of] $2,000. [To accept
> that] I think is really letting down all the writers
> that have gone before you as well. You know, I think
> they have all fought to have [writing] recognised as
> a legitimate profession. You don't do that for your

own fun. You do that to say, 'I want to spend my
life doing this. [...] I want to be that good. I want
people to pay $30, $40 a ticket to see what I have
to say.' Then I have to spend a considerable amount
of time [writing] something decent to say.

Playwright Brendan Cowell described an experience in
which, having been promised consultation throughout
the rehearsal process, he walked into a late rehearsal,
only to find that his play had become a musical and
that scenes he had thought emotionally-wrenching and
naturalistic were now being sung! Moreover, scenes
had been reorganised and, in his view, the play was
being satirised. But, as a young playwright, he was
unsure whether he should assert his legal rights:

Well, it was [...] too late, because there was a pre-
view the next night and lots of people really liked
it and thought it was funny and entertaining and
I was so young at that point. I'd just won my first
award and it was my first [...] play that was getting
out, getting beyond the fringe [...], so I didn't really
know my rights or know how much weight I could
throw around.

Given these fears, there is no doubt that the copyright framework is inherently incompatible with the
fluid nature of theatre creation, but what the current
framework does achieve is protection—for, as Rob
Brookman suggests, 'a group of artists [playwrights]
who must be the worst paid and treated in the world'.

Despite the fact that emerging playwrights believe
that the contribution they make, as the original
source of the work, should be recognised in copyright
law, those that I interviewed were acutely aware that

theatre is an inherently collaborative art form. I found no evidence of the 'precious' playwright vigilantly guarding every word. Alana Valentine put the point succinctly: 'If you were not open to collaboration, you would be a novelist. [… Y]ou have to believe that all those minds [directors, actors, designers etc.] are going to bring something incredible to the process and […] make it a richer, better thing.'

Distinguishing between the exception and the harmonious norm

There comes a moment, as the lights in the house go down and the curtain is about to rise on the first performance of a play, when the director hands the production over to the actors, usually with the words, 'It's yours now.' The martinet director used to find this the most painful moment of all. Playwrights experience a similar moment of hand-over, but, as Brendan Cowell observed, for them it occurs somewhat earlier in the process:

> There is definitely a moment when you have to hand your play over. […] I think it's really helpful for [actors] to hit the floor and it's nice for them to just be with the director and feel like they can go different places that maybe the writer didn't have […]. It's like the parents have gone away for the weekend [and] they've got the house to themselves. Then I think it's nice for the writer to come back in, when they're starting to run towards the end.

In a similar vein Tommy Murphy comments:

> D.H. Lawrence [said] something like, 'You need to
> trust in the tale not the teller.' I think that plays
> are good when they exist beyond the intentions of
> the author, when there is [...] something going on
> that's beyond me, beyond what I intended, [when]
> it has a life of its own [...]. For it to achieve that, I
> need to let go. I need to have another artist extend
> the work, to try and unearth those things, whether
> that other artist is a designer, director, actor.

Both Lawrence and Murphy are arguing that the true
creative work takes on an independent life that even
its creator cannot completely define or control. This
is no less true of a play than of a novel, of course—
perhaps much truer, given the number of people
required to bring a play text to life on a stage. But
the key word in Lawrence's motto has to be 'trust'.
Disputes between collaborators are easily avoided
under the current legislative framework, if there are
clear lines of communication between participants
and an atmosphere of harmony prevails during the
creation process. Griffin Theatre Company's director
Nick Marchand agreed: 'Most people will work to
ensure that conflict doesn't happen in the first place
and it does crop up very rarely. I mean there are
always going to be quibbles or minor disagreements
[...], but generally they are resolved by communication.'

Nor should it be assumed that, however much pain
it may cause him, a playwright is able to assert the
authority of his reading of his text, once the work is in
the hands of other collaborators and has passed into
the rehearsal room. This is no less true for established

writers than for new ones—even someone of David Williamson's stature.

> The picture of me as omnipotent, and able to order directors such as Wayne [Harrison] around at will, is far from the truth. Writers in theatre and film, even if they have impressive track records, are far less powerful than is often assumed. The critic John McCallum made an important point when he queried how lesser-known and starting playwrights could ever make their voices heard, given the nature of this power imbalance.[20]

In using Wayne Harrison as an illustration here, Williamson is referring to the dispute which flared up over Harrison's 1996 STC production of *Heretic*, his play about the intellectual conflict between Australian academic Derek Freeman and American anthropologist Margaret Mead. The playwright believed that the director had taken liberties with his script and that, for example, by adding 'Happy Birthday, Mister President', without authorisation, had turned Mead into a 1960s public icon in the mould of Marilyn Monroe and Jackie Kennedy—and committed a breach of ethical norms. The sin here, for Williamson, was that he believed he was not properly consulted. As long as they are consulted fully before, and during, the creation process, most writers appear to be open to the notion of bold interpretations of their work.

There are also numerous examples of notable playwrights who have sought to overcome the limitations of copyright law and formally acknowledge the contribution of non-writer collaborators. For example, in an afterword to the published text of his award-winning *Angels in America*, entitled 'With a Little Help from my Friends', American playwright Tony Kushner gave generous credit to all those who in 1993 had shared with him the task of bringing his extraordinary play to completion, and in particular his two dramaturgs—to whom he also paid 15 per cent of his royalties.[21] Such practices, said Kushner, were 'instructed through ten years and more of pitched battles over intellectual ownership and giving people credit'.[22] Here in Australia, the late Nick Enright adopted a similar philosophy with regard to his teenage play *A Property of the Clan* (1992), the material of which director Wayne Harrison and the STC took considerable pains to rework into a young-adult play *Blackrock* (1995). When the resultant 1997 film version of the play was contracted, its producer refused to pay a royalty to the STC collaborators; so Enright stepped in and paid them out of his writer's royalty.[23]

Similarly, there are examples of established playwrights who are happy to encourage theatre practitioners in their efforts to realise new readings of their work. When young Australian producer Nicole da Silva approached David Mamet's Sydney agent for permission to stage his two-hander, *Life in the Theatre*, intending to cast two females in roles originally written for men, her request was politely rejected. Undeterred, she wrote directly to the playwright. Within a fortnight, Mamet replied, through the same Sydney agent, saying 'I love it, do it, big thumbs up'.[24]

And in 2004 Currency Press published the dramatisation of Robert Dessaix's novel, *Night Letters*. In notes following the text, playwright Susan Rogers and Chris Drummond, who had directed the original production, acknowledge 'the long list of people who ha[d] played pivotal roles in the development of [the play]'. Despite having been the author of 'thousands of pages of writing' over the four-and-a-half years of gestation, Rogers made no proprietorial claim on the final text and shared with Drummond the extraordinary by-line, 'by Writer Susan Rogers and Director Chris Drummond'. Moreover, in tacit acknowledgement of Lawrence's motto, they also speak of Dessaix's 'fearless generosity and commitment to [their] essential creative freedom'; and of the 'trust' the novelist was prepared to place in their theatrical vision.[25]

But in none of these cases has the playwright's generosity succeeding in bringing about any modification of the copyright law. The fact is that the present legislation is essentially a harmonious framework, and to formally extend copyright protection to non-writer collaborators is to open a fearful can of worms. Most obviously, unless the author can negotiate a larger slice of income, to extend authorship to other collaborators is to cut into the playwright's royalties and erode further their already perilous financial position. It is undeniable that the current copyright framework has limitations, but, importantly, it does shield the playwright from numerous external challenges. I shall return to these issues, but first we must consider what Albee calls the 'interpretative act'.

3

Collaborators and the 'Interpretative Act'

In cases of new play development, however, the present rigid requirements of copyright law may not adequately equip it to identify the true nature of authorship.[26] As the experience of Lynn Thomson, the dramaturg on *Rent* demonstrated, the claims of writer-collaborators are hard enough to defend. I want here to consider some of the more problematic issues for non-writer collaborators when working with a copyright system framed around notions of the fixed and permanent.

As previously mentioned, unlike the playwright in text-based drama whose financial reward is an ongoing royalty, should her work achieve further productions—or be adapted into other forms, such as a film or a musical—those non-writer collaborators, whose contribution to the original process of staging the play is undeniably considerable, are rewarded by a fixed wage or upfront fee.

The idea that a collaboratively-based 'theatrical' right, acknowledging the contribution of non-writers, should replace the logo-centric framework that gives the playwright exclusive protection, is not new to legal commentators.[27] Almost a decade before Matthew Rimmer, senior lecturer at the ANU College of Law, argued that 'the director, the producers, the performers and the designer' need to be recognised as collaborators,[28] Marett Leiboff, who teaches at the University of Wollongong, had suggested in 1993 that much good might be served by trying to create a new right under copyright legislation exclusively for the theatrical community.[29] Wayne Harrison speaks for many directors—Chris Drummond and Andrew Ross, to name but two—in believing that 'the playwright, the director and the dramaturg should be considered to be the joint authors of a dramatic work'.[30] In the case of *Rent*, the court conceded that 'the letter of the law does not align completely with what may be just'.[31]

Does it really need repeating that theatre is never the creation of a single intelligence? Actors need considerable offstage help to bring about an act of theatre, never mind the indispensable presence of an audience. Some forms of theatre dispense with texts altogether, and in others a playwright's role might be limited to that of an amanuensis who records and shapes what a group of collaborators have imagined. As Tom Wright has said, it is not always easy to determine where one person's contribution ends and another's begins:

> In the course of one year I've worked as a dramaturg, as a director, as a playwright and as an actor […], all under different understandings of those terms. It's fine as long as the delineations are clear, but there are circumstances where the exact nature of your role within a production doesn't fall neatly into

> those baskets [...] and increasingly theatre's being made in that fashion. [It] has been for a while now and it leads to all sorts of problems.

Formal acknowledgment of the contribution of non-writer collaborators would have a significant impact on the theatre community, he believes:

> The idea of a theatrical right is something that would have served very well a number of auteurist practitioners in Western Europe in the post-war era. I'd be happy to imagine such an idea. [But] I suspect that theatrical rights would prove to be a Trojan horse—a neat horse for the final destruction of a logocentric [copyright] system.

Not surprisingly perhaps, John Frost, as a producer of commercial musical theatre, an art form that necessitates a rather wider collaborative effort, believes it unrealistic for playwrights to imagine they can command the kind of economic control they used to enjoy:

> The days when playwrights can ask for ten per cent of the gross [are] way gone. Certainly, in the commercial field you would never pay that. It would be maybe an exception if they really pushed it, but you just can't make it work financially. [...] I imagine David Williamson would be still [on] ten per cent. [But] Sydney Theatre Company is living in a bygone era. [They] should shake the tree because they could save some more money: no one else is going to produce this stuff other than state companies.[32]

Frost goes so far as to add his own name, or his role as producer, to the list of non-writer collaborators who might have a hand in the developmental process—to the extent of seeing the producer as co-author:

> I would certainly want a hands-on input into the construction and the writing of [an original work] and I would want to sit down with the author after he's done a first draft along with the director, if the director's on board, to actually work through that script. So if there were points in it that I was unhappy with I would want to change it to what I [thought] was right for the show.

What might be the result, were Frost's views regarding commercial musical theatre to filter into the non-profit sector of the Australian theatre, as indeed they have—though not without some resistance—in the United States?

Some practical limitations of the current framework

Copyright law's notion of 'fixed' may not be part of an artist's vocabulary. 'I work with people who understand the rougher nature of theatre', says Ben Winspear, 'and who are willing to make changes and sacrifices for the sake of theatricality:

> I haven't got a pedantic notion of theatre. [...] I don't think there is ever such a thing as a finished theatrical text. The only real theatre text is the act of the performance. The idea [of theatre as being fixed] has largely come about through scholars studying Shakespeare and trying to turn plays into literature. I find that really abhorrent. [... A] theatrical text is like an architect's plans. There wouldn't be a

> single building in the world that accurately reflects the [original] plans of an architect. You are always shaving off a bit here, and knocking an extra doorway through there [...]. I've been to performances in Berlin where they provide you with the text as a program and you can see all the crossings out and additions and changes. They give you a working version of the text so you can see just what they've done and where they've come from.

Nor is it easy to pinpoint with precision the moment at which either a play or a production can be regarded as having been finalised, and therefore 'fixed'. In the case of new work, which is often—if not invariably—in a state of revision and development, both during and beyond the rehearsal period, this is even more difficult. A situation such as this, indeed any element of fluidity, renders the task of drawing up clear and unambiguous legal guidelines difficult. This was a key factor in the failure of Lynn Thomson's claim to joint-authorship of *Rent*: the US *Copyright Act* defines a joint work as one 'prepared by two or more authors *with the intention that* their contributions be merged into inseparable and interdependent parts of a unitary whole'.[33] Can one always know *in advance* the moment at which and/or the extent to which collaboration will become necessary?

Copyright law's emphasis on the need for a 'fixed' text effectively denies non-writer collaborators any claim to original authorship of a dramatic work created by an individual, independently of others involved in a production. While the work of a film director is capable of reaching a definitive, permanent form—though who's to say whether that is the first cut, the commercial-release cut or the director's cut?—limits are less easily set on the work of a theatre director. Indeed, the theatre reviewer is faced each night with the difficulty of allotting praise or blame to participants in the performance. Such matters as a production's style, pace, overall 'feel' and clarity of purpose, for example, are incapable of being defined, and no protection is provided for the director's vision, style or method—or for those matters that are dictated by them.

In late 2005, for example, after he had worked unpaid for two months as director of the Broadway production of her *Tam Lin*, playwright Nancy McCleman fired Edward Einhorn on the grounds that he had made revisions to her original instructions regarding choreography and blocking. He had changed 'Exit' to 'Exit left', for example, 'Picks up book' to 'Picks up red book'. He filed a complaint, claiming ownership of copyright in his revisions and infringement of this right in the dramatist's use of them in subsequent performances. '[B]locking can be as complex and infinite as the possibilities of movement', he explained:

> Plays do not consist of mere exits and entrances, they consist of a constant flow of bodies from place to place and from position to position. The way the actors are placed, the position they are in, how long they stay there—all these things create pictures, and all those pictures create a mass of information. [...] Scenes staged in different ways can convey totally different moods and ideas, even with the same text.[34]

Einhorn's claim was ultimately unsuccessful and the US District Federal Court did not make a determination on the copyright issue. However, the Court commented in *dicta*: '[E]ven if [Einhorn] satisfies fixation, originality, and his work is found to be an expression, his "work" most likely will be viewed as a derivative work since it is a modification of the playwright's pre-existing stage instructions.'[35] This, of course, is precisely what Albee meant by an 'interpretative', as opposed to a 'creative', act. While the inability to protect the director's work may be dismissed as the unfortunate result of necessary line-drawing (between playwright and director), the impact a director has on a work, by bringing it to final performance, is clearly too significant to be ignored.

Providing non-writer collaborators with explicit copyright protection would represent a dramatic change in the copyright landscape. In Australia, efforts have been made to accord greater recognition to the work of the director. Tom Wright recalls the 1980s and '90s as a period when directorial 'ownership' became a contested issue, a period when 'directors saw themselves as the primary auteur voice and came to seek to impose their own reading on texts and productions [...]. Now, when that was felicitous to both parties, it was clearly not an issue. But occasionally it was going to cause conflict.'

Implying these movements might be cyclical—particularly in the larger state companies—Wright continues:

> Robyn Nevin [former Artistic Director of STC] would see herself as serving the playwright, the playwright's voice, and where she felt she was in

any danger of departing from that and departing from the intent of the playwright she would seek to communicate with the playwright.[36]

Indeed, even though Wayne Harrison was at the coalface of the *Heretic* controversy, he rejected any suggestion that he had 'gone to bat for the primacy of the director. [...] The decade-long Elizabethan Experiment series [he] conducted with [University of New South Wales academic] Dr Philip Parsons was intended to be a major corrective to directors' theatre.'[37]

So, where does this leave the director, who makes a significant contribution to the production, who has, together with the actors *et al.*, 'created the production', but fails to enjoy the benefits of the writer in copyright law? It is getting harder and harder to make a living out of directing, says Winspear. The director needs to be cut into a share of the royalties:

> I certainly think that without a level of return on a production it's probably just about impossible to make a living as a director. [...] It's so incredibly poorly paid, the opportunities are so few and so far between and quite often so dissatisfying and you are put under so much pressure. [...] I think it's a really frustrating experience to look around at a full house, know that a massive percentage of that money is going directly back to the company [and that] very little of it is going to the people whose work has gone into creating the piece in the first place.

In the view of Gale Edwards, who has extensive experience, both here and overseas, of staging new musical-theatre work, the director can face inequities because of a misunderstanding in Australia of the way in which musical theatre is created. In lyric theatre, she argues, the director is the driving force, the 'author':

> When *Les Miserables* was put to [director] Trevor [Nunn] by [producer] Cameron Mackintosh, it had been a concert in Paris, [...] a collection of songs, some of them great and some of them not so good. Cameron saw the potential of this, took it to Trevor Nunn and said, 'Will you develop this?' [...] There was no dialogue in *Les Miserables*, but it did mean following a big narrative that Trevor was in control of. So he threw out some of the songs and he needed more songs to be written. There is no doubt that unofficially—and this is my opinion—Trevor Nunn [the director, with John Caird, his co-adapter] wrote *Les Miserables*.

Although Nunn was not formally recognised as the author of the book of the musical, Edwards believes that his contribution was recognised financially and that he received a significant royalty for all future productions. In the US and Europe, she goes on, this financial acknowledgement of the director's contribution is an embedded industry practice:

> In Australia, we have had no precedent like that, so when my contracts are made [with producers] there isn't a real understanding of how musicals work and therefore I receive a standard commission as a director. Now there is a great folly in that because it doesn't acknowledge the specific role of a director creating a brand new musical work.

In Edwards's view directing a new musical work is more demanding than directing a film:

[T]he gestation period can be [...] longer, but it is certainly at least eighteen months of really hard work [before...] an intense rehearsal and technical period, so it's not like directing a play. [...I]f you are doing a $5 million musical you haven't got time to sit down for half a day and discuss it, [whether] this scene needs to be shorter, this needs to say this, this needs to say that. It's go, go, go! [...]. The writer must ultimately be subject to a creative vision that a Hal Prince or a Trevor Nunn has historically brought to the creation of Broadway and West End musicals. [...] Now if the writer is sitting right next to you and able to pen it off in five seconds, then it's in. But if it's not there by eight o'clock the next morning, you've got to write it yourself [...]. So if that means improvising a scene with the actors or doing whatever you can do to get it on. That's what you have to do.

The writer is not always sitting in the rehearsal room, of course. Even if she is, she might find it difficult to create deathless prose under such circumstances. My point is that the play as it ends up on the stage may well be markedly different from the one delivered by the playwright at the beginning of rehearsals. Gale Edwards spoke of a new work that she once directed, of which, she maintains, 600 of the 650 lines of text heard by the first-night audience had been contributed during rehearsals, primarily by herself! As no prior agreement had been reached to make her a joint author, she received none of the copyright author's financial rewards. Should the subsequent stage life of, say, a new musical involve a successful national, or international, tour, then the financial loss to the director could be very significant indeed. 'The income from [some of the shows I have directed] would have totally altered the next twenty years of my life', says Edwards, 'So I feel that this is a very powerful and important and unjust area.'

4

Further entrenchment: the copyright extension

O ne issue that prompted sharp reaction from my interviewees was the potential impact of the Australia-United States Free Trade Agreement, which came into force in January 2005. The amendments to copyright law under the terms of this agreement, which extended copyright protection of written work from 50 to 70 years after the death of the author,[38] entrench the individual-author narrative in law even more firmly than before.

The rights of the Bertolt Brecht Estate illustrate graphically the implications of this reform. Under the pre-amended law Brecht's plays—he died in 1956— would have come into the public domain in 2006. The extension enables the Brecht Estate to control them until 2026, a further seventeen years.

Other problems have been created by an extension of the copyright-protection period. Nick Marchand states that, in the absence of a theatre-specific copyright-collecting agency, it is up to theatre companies to locate and obtain clearances for material from playwrights or from the estates of dead playwrights. This can be an expensive and time-consuming task:

> Most of the time you [have] to deal directly with the trustees or the trustees' agent. This can mean lengthy delays, and a number of opinions com[ing] into play, [opinions] that might not [have been] quite so vociferous, [had they] come from the living playwright! The US tends to be much more protective than the rest of the world.

A further concern is that a particularly protective estate will be able to put their 'dead hand' on a playwright's work for a further 20 years. It will be the *estate* of the playwright, not the playwright herself, who will be able to restrict the creation of innovative productions.

Lurking in the opening-night audience of Company B's 2003 Sydney Festival production of Samuel Beckett's *Waiting for Godot* was an 'autocratic literary bulldog', ready to pounce.[39] The playwright's nephew and executor, Edward Beckett, threatened to take legal action against Company B for a breach of contract on the grounds that director Neil Armfield had used unauthorised music in the production. Armfield's reaction, defending theatre-making as a collaborative venture and querying the sacredness of classic texts, was delivered at a Beckett symposium, of which his production was a feature:

> In coming here with its narrow prescriptions, its dead controlling hand, the Beckett Estate seems to me to be the enemy of art. [...] If there is something to hope for at this watershed fiftieth anniversary of the play [...], it is that Edward gives his uncle's work back to artists who work with it. Let it go. Because if he doesn't, he is consigning it to a slow death by a thousand hacks.[40]

In relation to this dispute, Rachel Healy comments:

> I think that [...] the issue rests on what right an estate's representative might have to try and control the way that a play is performed. Plays are very unlike novels or [poems, for example]: they rest on collaboration with real live human beings in a room, all of whom are artists and have creative ideas and [...] years of experience in tackling the issues of the play and how you bring those issues to life theatrically.

And, as Rob Brookman describes, the *Act*'s extension of copyright control has impacted on the STC's programming choices:

> [Bernard Shaw's] *Major Barbara* was one year out of copyright when we did it. Ten per cent of box office on a show like *Major Barbara* is something like $80,000. For the STC that is a really, really significant sum of money. It's the difference between deciding to do a show and not doing it. So we do pay heed, quite significant heed, to where something falls. In the case of some other plays we are [currently] considering, I don't think there is any doubt that we'd [decide], 'Well, if we did this in two years' time, it would cost us $80,000 less.

Let's hold it over.' [...] So it is definitely something that, when you are watching the extension to 70 years, just makes life harder from our point of view.

On the other hand, Alana Valentine can see some justification for the extension, suggesting that only the 'genius' playwrights, those who deserve to be perpetuated, will be in a position to have their work performed 70 years after their death. Moreover, she asks rhetorically: why should a playwright be treated differently from a renowned visual artist, whose work would not be subjected to posthumous alteration?

It's about devaluing the work. [...] If paintings and sculptures have an inherent value then why doesn't a work of fiction? [...] My question to you is: Why is it so difficult to agree to the conditions of the estates? What's so restrictive that makes it impossible to keep to them? [I]f you don't want to do *Waiting for Godot* as Beckett wanted it, then why not do something else? I'm sure [I'm being] very controversial, but I just don't think an artistic free-for-all is realistic either. [...] Taking out bits [of *Waiting for Godot*] or putting in a whole lot of stuff is like cutting down [or adding to] a painting [by Picasso].

Problems with reform

There is a clear need for a more flexible and accommodating understanding of dramatic authorship. However, in concluding this part, I want to argue that formal reform, like the cinematographic copyright framework that explicitly acknowledges contributions by 'makers' of cinematographic works (inevitably producers) and directors in limited circumstances, may not necessarily be the most effective solution.

While acknowledging that 'discerning the author of a motion picture is far simpler than that of a theatre production', Devorah Katz wonders whether the work-for-hire doctrine, which is the dominant approach taken by the US film industry, might not constitute a way forward for theatre workers. Although 'the [film] production company [...] maintains the position as sole copyright owner, it implements a royalty structure so that an author receives a set amount of royalty payments for his employment and then an additional fee based on the amount of material he contributed to the end product.'[41] The implementation of this doctrine has not eliminated controversy from around the film designer's and writer's inability to obtain copyright interest in their work. It simply gives them access to greater recognition and remuneration. And it doesn't address the position of the non-writer collaborator.

To extend original ownership to multiple non-writer collaborators risks creating tensions in the rehearsal room that had not previously existed. Considering the fluid way in which a director works, granting her explicit original ownership rights might lead to even greater ambiguity and confusion when attempting to determine ownership. After all, blocking—the detailed positioning and movements of actors on the stage—is usually the result of negotiation between director and actors, as often as not these days initiated as much by what the actor feels to be appropriate as by what the director imposes. However reached, the ultimate decisions regarding blocking can rarely be regarded as the exclusive product of a director's intellectual labour.[42]

Therefore, while the director's contribution may be influential, the receipt of a royalty distribution at the expense of others, such as actors, may be no more than a system that protects no one but the playwright. How exactly might we quantify the respective contributions of each collaborator? And who is to decide the respective values of each? Not David Berthold, a director who does not believe his role equates with that of the author:

> I can't say that I would press for rights in a work and I guess that's because I see my role as being something different [...], shaping in the provision of ideas, occasionally suggesting a line [...]. Normally you [propose] a very bad version of the line, and this filters through the writer's imagination into something more [appropriate]. Mostly a director's contribution has to do with shaping the structure of [individual] scenes and the play [as a whole].

Among commercial producers there appears to be a greater desire to see innovative and flexible industry-contracting agreements develop in Australia along the lines of the Broadway contracting models. Gino Principe, Financial Director of Stage Entertainment UK, elaborates:

> You've got all these merging interests and there are different elements all associated with the production—producers, investors, copyright artists—but they have one thing in common. In order to make that production you've got to bring

all those elements together, so you've got to find commonality. I think [...] that what American authors tend to do is work in collaboration with the producers and acknowledge that it is a very expensive process to put together. A Broadway musical is going to cost you $10–$12 million US dollars before you start selling a ticket. So you start to see these rather creative arrangements about deferring royalties post recoupment, royalty pools, corridor arrangements and goodness knows what. This is what needs to happen more here.

The non-profit producers also believed there were pragmatic reasons for not extending ownership to non-writer collaborators such as producers and direc-tors. In practical terms, acknowledging more than one individual playwright could lead to incredibly complex arrangements. As the theatre industry has no specific copyright-collecting agency or -registration system, it would be an onerous task for subsequent producers to establish who to pay royalties to when a variety of collaborators claim original ownership. Rob Brookman thought that if you were to try and track input from every single person who had made a contribution and then try to reflect that in a re-calculated or shared royalty, it would turn into an administrative nightmare. Moreover, to formally expand original ownership to include more collabora-tors, was more likely to enhance, not reduce, tensions between collaborators:

> It could turn into a fairly toxic situation in the rehearsal room, [with] creators becom[ing] very, very defensive about their work, [... and] beginning

to fear that if significant changes were made, then their earnings might diminish dramatically.

David Berthold agrees: 'It's difficult enough a week after the workshop to remember who suggested what in the conversation, simply because it's a conversation involving five, ten, fifteen people in a room and getting collectively excited [about] an idea.'

Although Gale Edwards advocates greater protection for directors, she is not blind to the potential difficulties:

> [Y]ou are under such stress as a director that the last thing you do is look over your shoulder, going, 'Will someone count the number of lines in that scene? Did someone count that I actually wrote that line and the writer wrote those two lines? And the musical director threw in that line and actually the actor threw in that line but they were all following the director's brief which was that the scene should say xyz?'

Attempting to apportion ownership before the beginning of the preparation period could also pose problems for the way in which the work proceeds. What is agreed at the outset may not be in line with what is decided after the event. Most actors would confirm that what the writer gives to the actors at the outset rarely conforms exactly to what they deliver on opening night. Nonetheless, says Alana Valentine, even if he or she wrote no more than six lines of the 600 used in 'his' work as it finally reaches the stage, the playwright is still making a contribution that is worthy of protection:

> I think that there is still an argument that even if you bring a text, and only six lines of it end up in the play, that it was still the bringing of the text that

was the act of authorship. [...] A stage director can rewrite 99 per cent of the play as far as I'm concerned, but it's still [the playwright] who's offered the [play text] to be rewritten.

Once multiple collaborators have formal legal rights in the work, and parties are required to divide ownership legally, are not disputes bound to be inevitable?

5

Why Change?

Legislative reform that expressly acknowledges the rights of non-writer collaborators as original authors is not a way for ownership structures to develop in the foreseeable future. Reform is often justified by highlighting the isolated, but public, disputes, played out in the press, involving high-profile organisations and individuals. By focussing on the few instances of dispute, we too-easily make the assumption that all practitioners act exclusively out of self-interest. That is, that all playwrights vigilantly protect their works, all directors demand recognition of their contribution as creative under copyright law, and all producers seek ownership because they take significant risks in producing a new work.

There are three reasons why copyright reform may not be the best way to proceed, reasons that have not been given adequate consideration by the legal commentators who have advocated them. These reasons, however, must be understood with an important caveat in mind. We must proceed with caution in this debate when attempting to draw clearly-defined opposing positions. Edward Albee draws a distinction between the 'creative' and the 'interpretative' contribution. It is a useful distinction, and to adopt it simplifies life for the lawyer-maker, who prefers the 'fixed' to the 'fluid', the 'clear-cut' to the 'ill-defined'. But might not an actor or a director justifiably regard what they do as creative? (And is not the work of a designer 'fixed' and copyrightable?) To argue, as Albee does, that without the playwright's original work, the other collaborators would be dispensable, is to imply that what she does is of a completely different order from what they do. If it is true that actors, for example, are dependent on a playwright's text as the source of their creativity, that they need to be given a thought, an idea, an emotion to express; that they do not conjure their performances out of thin air—cannot playwrights be said to be equally dependent on pre-existing sources? Though it may not always be possible to identify these in the form of words on a printed page, surely a playwright's characters and plots invariably come from a source outside his own head? Shakespeare, Molière and Brecht—to name but three—would surely have agreed. But to proceed further with this argument is to open a Pandora's box wider than space here permits. Let me move on to my three reasons for maintaining the status quo in copyright law, being aware of the dangers in drawing neat opposing positions.

First, the risk of disrupting an otherwise harmonious working relationship between equals. In the limited ethnographic study I have conducted, there was no evidence that disputes over authorship were commonplace. Indeed, several interviewees stressed that if a dispute between collaborators did occur, it would be more the result of a breakdown over artistic matters rather than any inherent deficiency in the copyright framework. Commenting in the context of moral rights, David Berthold stated that the amendments to the law have had little or no impact on his work:

> [T]o actually take recourse over moral rights sounds to me like the production is in deep trouble and often the deep trouble can have to do with things that are beyond the notion of moral rights. Certainly [...], I can't see it making any difference to my practice.

There is clearly a risk that a new system would be more inequitable than the existing one.

Second, a reform agenda will inevitably impact on the vulnerable position of playwrights attempting to make a living from writing. Unless a greater share of box office can be negotiated, any allocation of royalties to non-writers must diminish the playwright's percentage—as Craig Lucas quickly discovered. It is undeniable that the current copyright framework has limitations, but it does shield the playwright from numerous external challenges including what is often a significant power imbalance between emerging writers and professional production companies. By shifting the legal framework from an individual to a communitarian norm, unfairness is just as likely to arise against individual-based creators. If unfairness is just as likely to arise in a different guise, then why bother to seek reform?

These attacks on the legitimacy of the playwright's legal rights are one of the latest attempts to disempower the 'individual author', as witnessed in other forms of creation. For example, US film, television and radio writers were compelled to take action, in what became known as the 2007–2008 Writer's Guild of America Strike, over what they saw as an inequity in the allocation of residuals for new technology media in comparison to the accepted practice of large American production companies. On the eve of the strike, writer Howard Michael Gould argued:

> Soon, when computers and your TV are connected, that's how we're all going to watch. Okay? Those residuals are going to go [...] towards zero, if we don't make a stand now. [...] I might have been the most moderate one up here when we started, but I sat there in the room the first day and they read us those thirty-two pages of rollbacks. And what they wanted us to hear was, 'If you don't give us what you [*sic*] want on the important thing, we're gonna come after you for all those other things.' But what I heard was, if we give them that thing, they'll *still* come after us for those other things. And in three years, it'll be, 'We want to revamp the whole residual system', and in another three years, it'll be, 'Y'know what, we don't really want to fund the health fund the way we've been.' And then it will be pension. And then it'll be credit determination. And there

just is that time when everybody has to see—this is
one where we just gotta stand our ground.[43]

The third reason why I regard reform as unjusti-
fied—one that is indirectly relevant to the first—is
that academic commentary overlooks the ability of
practitioners to successfully develop their own flexible
contractual-ownership structures within the current
framework when the need to acknowledge collaborative ownership arises. It is important to distinguish
between allowing collaborative arrangements to
develop more naturally by way of contractual relationships between like-minded parties—something which
should be encouraged—and compelling collaborators
to apportion ownership of original works through
the formal mechanism of the copyright system. Once
multiple parties are identified as having explicit rights
to original authorship, disputes will inevitably arise.

When examining the position of the individual
author as she operates in practice, the deficiencies of
the doctrinal framework are not as self-evident. Not
all playwrights are as hard-line on this issue as Edward
Albee, and some will voluntarily enter into collaborative projects, because they have a strong desire to
share ownership and to move beyond creating theatre
under the traditional logocentric model. As was noted
earlier, the published texts of *The Merry-Go-Round in
the Sea* and *Night Letters* name both playwright and
director as joint authors—in the latter case explicitly
referring to them as '*Writer* Susan Rogers and *Director*
Chris Drummond' (my emphasis).

The Australian Writers' Guild, being appreciative of
the collaborative nature of the creative process, offers

guidelines to writers at workshops on ways in which they should structure their arrangements under copyright law so as to acknowledge multiple contributions:

> There has prevailed a view [...] that workshops [...] are conducted solely for the benefit of the author. This view is misinformed and has most probably been the basis of situations where no payment is provided for writers of plays which are workshopped. In fact, it should be understood that workshops exist to further the mutual interests of not only the writer, but also theatrical companies, actors, stage crews, technical crews and audiences. A workshop is directed to the shaping of a play, the revealing of its flaws and strengths and the potential of its form for performance.[44]

Parties wishing to be acknowledged as contributors to the creative process should be permitted to negotiate the terms of their 'collaborative authorship' as the work develops. Under this arrangement there would be no need to reform copyright law to acknowledge non-writer collaborators as authors. In other words, the current copyright system is flexible enough to accommodate these arrangements.

Tom Wright believes that a flexible approach of this kind is needed and, indeed, that different forms of contractual arrangement will emerge as collaborative industry-contracting practices and custom evolve. The playwright might be prepared to trade away some of the benefits of being commissioned under a logocentric transaction. This would mean that the end-point of a commission ceases to be an 'authored script', but rather a 'theatrical production'. This is certainly what one (unidentified) theatre company in Melbourne appears to be proposing. As Wright understands it, 'the commissioning process and the contracting of writers [would] completely chang[e]':

> [I]t's based upon the idea that when you employ a writer, you employ them partly as a service provider, but partly as a collaborator of 'special significance', [as] someone who develops and sparks theatre. [...] So the distinction that's made about the 'word designer' (to use that awful neologism) is that the word designer's [i.e. playwright's] value is placed higher because they're required to create something out of nothing. [... A team of individuals], the director, a writer, in some cases a designer, in some cases [...] an actor, are all being commissioned under *similar agreements* to develop a work, allowing for their individual skills.
>
> [T]hat to a certain extent downgrades the idea [of] the writer [as] someone who sits in a garret in front of a Mac and comes up with a blueprint for theatre. [... A]nd it downgrades that idea that the writer [...] owns the work which then is handed over to someone else. But [it does create] a greater likelihood that the end-point is theatre and not script. [...] I would personally be quite happy with such a model and I suspect a number of younger playwrights [...] might be prepared to embrace it too. But I'm sure there are also many young and emerging writers who are far happier with the standard ten per cent of takings.

Wright's is a model in which the writer is only one member of a team of collaborators, all having equal 'special significance'. Each team-member, whether he is writer, director, actor, designer or dramaturg, would be commissioned under similar agreements and share ownership of the original work. Despite the Guild's acknowledgement of group-devised work, Rachel Healy was not confident that it would lead anywhere:

> I'd be very interested to hear the Australian Writers' Guild's response to [any suggestion regarding a shared arrangement], because they have always been absolutely adamant that the playwright should receive no less than ten per cent. I think that if [such contractual developments occurred] it would be a very, very big thing to happen.

This essay has identified the need to reconsider the merits of the logocentric copyright system as it currently applies to theatre. In law and in literary theory, commentators have criticised the copyright framework because of its celebration of the author function, where the 'original author' of the text is accorded the exclusive rights to the dramatic work. This conventional analysis fails to appreciate the plurality of legal relations and different distributions of power that exist in practice. This plurality can best be understood by applying methods such as ethnography, that are under-utilised in legal research.

The plurality of law, that has undermined the position of the playwright, is not a recent phenomenon. Nineteenth-century commercial licensing arrangements in the theatre were pioneered by the entrepreneurial efforts of the likes of Samuel French in the United States and Thomas Hailes Lacy in Britain. While copyright affords rights to the original author of text-based dramatic work, in 1830 Samuel French came up with an extraordinarily profitable idea:

> He would license from the authors of plays of proven popularity the rights both to publish […] acting editions of those plays, so that each actor could have a full script to work from, and to sub-license the performing rights for those plays to amateur groups and provincial professional companies, keeping a healthy commission from the royalties collected for the authors.[45]

Viewed from this contextualised battlefield, as many of my interviewees implied, the apparently privileged position of the individual author may, by the application of legal doctrine, prove to be a myth in practice.

Endnotes

1 Recorded and transcribed by the author in April 1992, at the Inge Festival, Independence, Kansas. They are reproduced in Jeane Luere (ed.), *Playwright versus Director: Authorial Intentions and Performance Interpretations* (Westport, Connecticut: Greenwood Press, 1994), p. 49–50.

2 See Luere (ed.), p. 140.

3 Private conversation in Sydney with editor John Golder, 1 July 2009.

4 Hereafter either the *Copyright Act* or the *Act*.

5 *Copyright Act* s 35 (2).

6 See Jacklyn (Marett) Leiboff, 'Actors, Directors and Others and Writers: Copyright Protection for Non-Writer Contributors in Group-Devised Theatre', *Arts & Entertainment Law Review* (October 1993), pp. 13–15.

7 The term is Jacklynn (Marett) Leiboff's.

8 *Copyright Act*, s 31 (1).

9 *Copyright Act*, s 35 (2).

10 See Matthew Rimmer's '*Heretic*: Copyright Law and Dramatic Works', *Queensland University of Technology Law and Justice Journal*, 2:1 (2002), pp. 131–49 and the same author's, 'Damned to Fame: The Moral Rights of the Beckett Estate', *Incite*, 24:5 (2003), available at http://alia.org.au/publishing/incite/2003/05/beckett. html (accessed 20 July 2009).

11 The long list of US scholarship includes Douglas Nevin, 'No Business Like Show Business: Copyright Law,

the Theatre Industry and the Dilemma of Rewarding Collaboration', *Emory Law Journal*, 53 (2004), pp. 1553–70; T. Yellin, 'New Directions for Copyright: The Property Rights of Stage Directors', *Columbia VLA JL and Arts*, 24 (2001), pp. 317–47; Susan Keller, 'Collaboration on Theatre: Problems and Copyright Solutions', *UCLA Law Review*, 33 (1986), pp. 891–939; Laura Lape, 'A Narrow View of Creative Cooperation: The Current State of Joint Work Doctrine', *Albany Law Review*, 61 (1997), pp. 43–84; Jane Lee, 'Upstaging the Playwright: The Joint Authorship Entanglement Between Dramaturgs and Playwrights', *Loyola LA Entertainment Law Journal*, 19 (1998), pp. 75–106; Paulette Fox, 'Preserving the Collaborative Spirit of American Theatre: The Need for a Joint Authorship Rule in Light of the *Rent* Decision's Unanswered Questions', *Cardozo Arts and Entertainment Law Journal*, 19 (2001), pp. 497–531; Beth Freemal, 'Theatre, Stage Directions and Copyright Law', *Chicago Kent Law Review*, 71 (1996), pp. 1017–40.

12   In Australia see Rimmer, '*Heretic*: Copyright Law and Dramatic Works'; Leiboff, 'Actors, Directors and Others and Writers'; Victoria Paellicano, 'Dance and Copyright: Pas de Deux or Pas de Disaster?', *Media and Arts Law Review*, 2 (1997), pp. 116–34 (dance context); Stephen Rebikoff, 'Restructuring the Test for Copyright Infringement in Relation to Literary and Dramatic Plots', *Melbourne University Law Review*, 25 (2001), pp. 340–73; W. Ling-Chan, 'The Writer is King: Copyright in Devised Theatre', *Art + Law*, (June 2004), p. 10.

13   For a comprehensive examination of both disputes, see Matthew Rimmer articles cited above.

14   See Joy Goodwin, 'Far From the Spotlight, a Brewing Fight Over Theatrical Rights', the *New York Times*, 22 November 2008, C3.

15   Richard Nelson, '2007 Laura Pels Keynote Address', at Curtain Call, the annual meeting of the Alliance of Resident Theatres/New York (A.R.T./New York, April 9, 2007), available at www.art-newyork.org/index.php/events/annualmgt/am-2007/ (accessed 5 April 2009).

16   See, for example, Jonathan Bates, *The Genius of Shakespeare* (New York: OUP, 1997), John Fuegi, *Brecht and Company: Sex, Politics and the Making of Modern Drama* (New York: Grove, 1994); Steve Giles, *Bertolt Brecht and Critical Theory: Marxism, Modernity and the Threepenny Lawsuit* (Bern: Lang, 1997); James Knowlson, *Damned to Fame: A Life of Samuel Beckett* (London: Bloomsbury, 1997); Stephen Hinton (ed.), *Kurt Weill: The Threepenny Opera*, 2nd ed. (London: Cambridge University Press, 2000); Brian Kiernan, *David Williamson: A Writer's Career* (Sydney: Currency Press, 1996).

17   Lionel Bently, 'Copyright and the Death of the Author in Literature and Law', *Modern Law Review*, 57 (1994), p. 981.

18   'Creation as Collaboration: Looking at Joint Authorship in Theater Production' (2008), available at http://www.iposgoode.ca/wp-content/uploads/2008/10/creation-as-collaboration-looking-at-joint-authorship-in-theater-production/ (accessed 25 July 2009).

19   August Baker *et al.*, 'An Author is an Author is an Author: Collaborators Don't Own a Play, Declares a Cadre of Playwrights', *American Theatre*, 15: 6 (1998), p. 6.

20   David Williamson, 'Some Like it Hot ... But I Don't', *Sydney Morning Herald*, 9 April 1996, quoted by Rimmer, '*Heretic*', p. 132.

21   Rimmer, '*Heretic*', p. 140.

22   Quoted in 'Tony Kushner's *Angels*', in *Dramaturgy in American Theatre: A Source Book* , ed. by Susan Jonas,

Geoff S. Proehl and Michael Lupu (New York: Harcourt Brace, 1997), p. 472.

23 See Rimmer, 'Heretic', p. 143.

24 Emily Dunn, 'Direct Approach Works for Tenacious Young Producer', *Sydney Morning Herald*, 22 November 2006.

25 Again, in 2006, when Currency Press published *The Merry-Go-Round in the Sea*, originally staged by Black Swan in Perth in 1997, the by-line read 'The play: Dickon Oxenburgh [writer] & Andrew Ross [director of the 1997 production]'.

26 See Lori Petruzzelli, 'Copyright Problems in Post-Modern Art', *Journal of Art and Entertainment Law*, 5 (1994), p. 115.

27 See the interesting recent work in America of, for example, Douglas M. Nevin, 'No Business Like Show Business: Copyright Law, the Theatre Industry and the Dilemma of Rewarding Collaboration', *Emory Law Journal*, 53: 3 (2004).

28 See Rimmer, '*Heretic*', p. 132.

29 See Leiboff, 'Actors, Directors and Others'.

30 See Rimmer, '*Heretic*', p 139. On Andrew Ross, see note 25 above.

31 At the district court level: *Thomson v Larson* 96 Civ 8876, 615, 729 (S.D.N.Y. 1997).

32 It should be remembered that Frost made these comments about the STC three years ago. They may no longer be valid.

33 *US Copyright Act* [2005] 17 U.S.C. § 101, cited by Katz (her emphasis).

34 Edward Einhorn, 'A Case for the Stage Director's Copyright', available at www.untitledtheater.com/DirectorsCopyright.htm (accessed 24 July 2006).

35 *Einhorn v Mergatroyd Productions* 426 F Supp 2d 189 (2006).

36   See, however, recent newspaper commentary: Elissa Blake, 'The Removalist: No Room at Wharf for My Stories', *Sydney Morning Herald*, 13 May 2009 and also Williamson's letter in reply, *Sydney Morning Herald*, 15 May 2009.

37   Rimmer, '*Heretic*', p. 134.

38   See *US Free Trade Agreement Implementation Act 2004* (Cth) Schd 9, Part 6: to amend, for example, the *Copyright Act* ss 33(2), 33(3) and 33(5),34(1), 81(2), 93, 94.

39   See Sharon Verghis, 'Waiting for Beckett Jnr: Bugger That for a Joke', *Sydney Morning Herald*, 10 January 2003.

40   See Verghis, 'Waiting for Beckett Jnr'.

41   'Creation as *Collaboration*', see note 18 above.

42   See Freemal, 'Theatre, Stage Directions and Copyright Law', p. 1026.

43   Howard Michael Gould, *Writer Speaks Out*, available at YouTube: www.youtube.com/watch?v=beMNePzqpzQ (accessed 4 July 2009).

44   The Guild recommends that the rewards of joint authorship 'need to be agreed [...] at the pre-material stage', available at http://www.ozscript.org/rates.php (accessed 21 July 2009).

45   Kevin N. Scott, 'Who Owns the Rights? Copyright, the Law and Licensing the Show', *Teaching Theatre*, 10:4 (1999), p. 7.

Readers' Forum

Responses to Robert Walker's *Beethoven or Britney? The Great Divide in Music Education.*

Margaret Bradley is Senior Curriculum Advisor/ Music Advisor, Curriculum K–12, NSW Department of Education and Training.

Listening to Britney may lead to, or from, listening to Beethoven, so music educators often use both as teaching resources rather than one or the other. We live in a world where a wide range of music is enjoyed by a wide range of people in an even wider range of settings, styles and modes. Much of the material in this musical melting pot can be traced back to its roots in Pythagorean theory, yet it also includes music of our time which will always challenge the notion of what has constituted a rigorous music education up to now.

In Australia we inhabit a unique position with regard to the way in which we experience music. Recently I was in the Opera Theatre of the Sydney Opera House, listening to operatic overtures by an Algerian from Paris. I often sit in the fourth row of the stalls and watch the Australian Ballet weave its magic to the accompaniment of a chamber orchestra, but this was different. It was the audience that was dancing. The way we respond to music varies with age and yet here was a mixed audience embodying their response through movement.

The idea that music education in this country has been damaged by a wave of sociological theory in education is untrue, particularly with regard to music education in New South Wales. Hundreds of specialist music teachers work hard to deliver a quality music education and support students in a myriad of ways. Recent reports show the rise in students' interest in music rather than sport, and in numbers of students sitting HSC Music exams and enrolling in music courses.

Strategies are needed to improve and update the pre-service training offered in the tertiary sector in order to support the realities of the music classroom in this century and address rapid technological development and changes in educational delivery.

Music education in the twenty-first century continues to be underpinned by pedagogies espoused by music educators worldwide and yet these models for teaching music in the Western art tradition need reinvigorating to engage and continue to inspire a new generation of musicians in a global community. Recent initiatives such as partnerships between artists and teachers in schools will enhance the teaching and learning on both sides.

Music education not only supports brain-stem development but enhances other areas of learning. Having returned to the Sydney Opera House Concert Hall recently to view the Department of Education and Training's Instrumental Festival, I couldn't help but be surprised by the comments arising from the audience such as, 'I never thought recorders on mass could sound that good.' The massed string and recorder players performed with confidence and vigour. During the rehearsal process primary students developed discipline and focus to perform in unison and showcased their talents alongside those of their dedicated teachers.

Music is alive and well in the public sector and proudly reflects a kaleidoscope of styles and experiences with a diverse range of students and teachers. Primary and secondary schools in NSW are providing a significant contribution to the lives of these students and their future music education in Australia.

Elissa Milne is a specialist in the composition of educational piano music, which has been included in syllabuses around the world. She is published by Faber Music and Hal Leonard Australia and recently created a new pre-preliminary syllabus for the AMEB to be introduced in 2010.

Robert Walker's essay got it right in so many regards. Yes, there *is* a correlation between appropriate resources and appropriate opportunities in music education, and most students in Australia get neither. Yes, primary school students typically receive music education from musical illiterates. Yes, students gain benefits from learning to *play* musical instruments, not from learning *about* them. Yes, Britney and Beethoven are *not* commensurate musical, cultural or intellectual experiences.

But then there are the ways in which this essay got it so very wrong.

The claim that Western classical music is the most advanced (read 'valuable') musical culture on earth is made via some flimsy manipulation of anecdote and statistics (lots of people in China learn to play Western classical music, therefore they are disdainful of Chinese music traditions, therefore Western classical music trumps Chinese opera). As well there are smoke and mirrors based on some old-fashioned notions of what makes classical music great (the use of numerical relationships based on the golden section in late eighteenth-century composition). Dr Walker compounds this by stating that only Western art music is capable of expressing individual emotion.

That Dr Walker fails to take into account the sociological factors for Western music's ascendancy in Asia is not surprising, as he appears to discount the entire discipline of sociology. That he appears to restrict Western art music to musical examples based on the golden section is perhaps more astonishing, for this eliminates much of the canon and lays the foundation for many aspects of Western art music to remain unstudied unless they can be shown to connect to this mathematical principle. That he believes that individual emotion cannot be expressed via any other musical tradition speaks more about Dr Walker's view of human psychology than it does about the musical traditions of the world.

The facts are that learning to play a musical instrument has been demonstrated to improve brain function by around seven IQ points for as long as the person continues to play their instrument; and that keyboard instruments get the best results in this IQ advantage. There is a growing body of work demonstrating how musical performance experiences (both public and private) bolster self-esteem and facilitate self-expression—key elements in maintaining good mental health. These findings are of particular interest in a culture where so many teenagers find self-harm the most effective means of communicating their anxieties, and where the economy relies on low-level self-loathing as a catalyst to consume.

The latest Australian Bureau of Statistics report into children's participation in activities after school shows that children coming from English-speaking homes are significantly more likely to be involved in activities like music and sport outside of the school environment. Not only are the music education resources in the education system reserved for the lucky and the well-resourced, but privately-obtained music education is also the preserve of those with the greatest social capital.

Dr Walker identifies that changes in educational strategies in the past were intended to redress some of this imbalance, but instead students were left free of grammatical skills (for example) at the end of their education. This has had a correlation in music education, where students can take hours of music classes at school and simply listen to pop music or watch until the compulsory hours are up. But Dr Walker is wrong to put the blame squarely on the shifts in educational fashion.

Because of the disparity in private musical education from one student to another, because of its one-on-one nature, and because students are able to progress entirely at their own pace (as compared to the pace of their age-based cohort), by the time classroom music teachers begin to address musical literacy (literally, being able to read music) the class is already hopelessly unevenly assembled. Children immediately fall into two camps, one feeling stupid and overwhelmed by this incomprehensible new world the teacher is whisking them through, and the other bored by this revision of basics they mastered years ago.

Australia's education system has no means of dealing with skills best taught one-on-one, and no strategies for allowing students to progress at a different pace from their peers. This is in complete contrast to the massive private music education industry, where one-on-one tuition is the norm, and students (mostly) recognise that progress is connected to their effort, not to the passage of time. The review Dr Walker is critiquing does not address this systemic incompatibility in the provision of music education, and he does not take the time to tease out this structural weakness. He does, however, conclude his essay by calling for a requirement that students study set musical works from the Western art music canon. He argues this on the basis that Western art music is best, that it is our cultural heritage, and that a student's education is impoverished by the exclusion of Western art music. On the second two points I concur, but I would add another reason for works (from any musical tradition) to be set for study: by studying the same musical works across the nation, students can begin to have a conversation with each other, beyond the fences of their state or private schools, and across the geographical divides that the internet (but not the curriculum) has made meaningless.

Mandating that the study of music include a substantial Western art music component needs to be balanced by the recognition that music *is* also a commodity. Part of a student's music education *ought* to involve an examination of the way music has acquired value of a monetary as well as a cultural kind. It is naïve (let alone anachronistic) to believe that the primary musical engagement experienced by Australians is performative, not one of consumption. When we teach students how music (and all kinds of music) works, we equip them to experience music as musicians, not simply as customers.

Dean Biron is a Brisbane-based independent scholar. His PhD thesis, completed at the University of New England, was entitled 'Contemporary Music and its Audiences.'

Robert Walker's essay on the present state of music education in this country is both passionately expressed and enlightening. He articulates well the need for music educators to be knowledgeable and supported by adequate resources, and cites numerous compelling studies which reinforce the value of learning music from a young age. There are, however, several key aspects to his argument that invite response.

The first is encapsulated in his chosen title, *Beethoven or Britney?* Those attentive to recent episodes in Australia's so-called culture wars will have come across this style of language before, in countless jeremiads on English studies deteriorating to the point where comic books and shopping lists are valued as highly as Shakespeare and Dickens. Such false dichotomies only obfuscate the situation in literature, so it is disappointing to see one given headline status in the corresponding discussion in music. Surely there are enough anti-dialectical debates being propagated through the media (climate-change advocates versus climate-change sceptics, and so forth) without intellectuals encouraging more?

Walker here seeks to pass judgment on the sociological method and associated cultural studies field, two projects commonly united under the term postmodernism. Typically, postmodernism's detractors focus upon its more dubious traits (such as lack of depth, the celebration of populism), while choosing to ignore or downplay the positive ones (such as intertextuality, the softening of cultural divisions). The core issue, though, is whether the general widening of scope promoted under postmodernism necessarily equates to a 'dumbing down', as Walker and others assume.

The American educator Wilson Moses once observed that critics of the sociological method customarily refer to their quarry by way of 'the most grotesque and extreme examples'.[1] It can be added that nowadays advocates of contemporary mass culture are often found roundly embracing the same lowest-common-denominator cases. Yet serious devotees of classical music doubtless do not want their art represented only by the many commonplace, kitsch exemplars available—why should those who are serious about other forms of music be any different?

This brings me to another, closely-related issue, most clearly articulated in Walker's assertion that followers of rock and pop music are wrong to believe that 'this music [can] express feelings, emotions and psychological states as powerfully as any operatic aria'. In other words, according to Walker's argument, if it is not classical music, then it must be entertainment—and shallow entertainment at that. As well as being impossible to prove, such a claim truly is constantly being refuted by listeners (many autodidacts who would nonetheless shun the pejorative 'fan') experiencing the same kinds of powerful effects through non-classical music. I had yet another such encounter at the recent Liquid Architecture festival. The musician in question, the German Thomas Koner, managed the trick using only a laptop computer and a video screen, and as an added bonus his work totally befuddles the divide between classical and popular music precisely because it is neither.

Walker goes on to say that 'in rock 'n' roll meaning appears more in the gesture of the singer/dancer than in the music'. Once again, a lot of sociological and cultural-studies critics would have no argument with this. But, apart from the problem of explaining exactly what 'rock 'n' roll' means as a musical category in 2009, he has another hurdle to overcome before such an assertion can be verified. It is not possible to shove aside the exclusivity of art music—the only form of music that allegedly *is* expressed chiefly through sounds—so easily. Christopher Small, whom Walker cites, questions how it is that so many have unequivocally privileged, both aesthetically and ethically, a genre which is of concern to only a tiny minority within Western industrialised society.[2] I agree with Walker that ignorance about the history and methods of classical music is unfortunate; it is equally unfortunate that the same level of ignorance is commonly shown toward other types of music.

It is also a far from simple matter to separate off classical music from popular music in the first place. Between those two increasingly isolated poles is a vast middle ground, not even acknowledged by a majority of observers, who are too reliant upon the scant information with which television and radio provide them. Moreover, all of the arts are bound up with commercialism, classical music being no exception (for evidence of this check out *Limelight* magazine, that self-styled bastion of local high culture that is in truth the art music equivalent of *Smash Hits*). And the classical tradition, even more so than the pop/rock tradition, has long been a haven for conformity and nostalgia.[3] What is perhaps most interesting in contemporary music are the many alliances, experiments and contraventions that show these received traditions to be to some extent illusory.

One could add countless names to Walker's list of Australian musicians whose dedication and achievements show the value of a deep engagement with music at both a technical and philosophical level. Included would be many of the jazz-inflected composers and improvisers mentioned in Peter Rechniewski's recent Platform Paper,[4] each making thoughtful and complex music from somewhere beyond the Western art-music fortress, as well as numerous others working at the margins of pop/rock. There is plenty of evidence to suggest that a practical, theoretical and historical understanding of all the different forms of musical expression would best contribute to encouraging well-rounded, motivated, questioning students of diverse social and cultural circumstances.

1   'The Remaking of the Canon,' *Partisan Review*, 2 (1991), p. 369.

2   *Musicking: The Meanings of Performing and Listening* (Middletown, CT: Wesleyan University Press, 1998), p. 3.

3   For a discussion on this, see John Gingell and Ed Brandon, *In Defence of High Culture* (Oxford: Blackwell, 2001), pp. 69–84.

4   Peter Rechniewski, *The Permanent Underground: Australian Contemporary Jazz in the New Millennium*, Platform Papers 16 (Sydney: Currency House, 2008).

Subscribe to **Platform Papers**

Have the papers delivered quarterly to your door

4 issues for $60.00 including postage within Australia

The individual recommended retail price is $14.95.

___ I would like to subscribe to 4 issues of Platform Papers for $60.00

I would like my subscription to start from: ___ this issue (No. 22)

___ the next issue (No. 23)

Name_____

Address_____

_____

_____ State _____ Postcode _____

Email _____

Telephone _____

Please make cheques payable to Currency House Inc.

Or charge: ___ Mastercard ___ Visa

Card no. ___ ___ ___ ___ ___ ___ ___ ___ ___ ___ ___ ___

___ ___ ___ ___

Expiry date _____ Signature _____

CURRENCY HOUSE

Fax this form to Currency House Inc. at: 02 9319 3649

Or post to: Currency House Inc., PO Box 2270, Strawberry Hills NSW 2012 Australia